The Spanish Traditional Cookbook

Food, Flavors, and Recipes of Spain

CULTURAL CUISINE BOOKS

Melania Yakob

Introduction

Welcome to a culinary journey through the rich and diverse Spanish gastronomy. Spain, a land of passion and tradition, offers us a delicious variety of dishes that reflect its history, geography and vibrant culture. From the coasts bathed by the Mediterranean Sea to the Cantabrian Mountains of the north, each region offers unique flavors and unforgettable gastronomic experiences.

In this book, we've compiled a careful selection of authentic recipes, from classics like paella and potato omelette to lesser- known but equally delicious culinary gems. Each dish has been carefully chosen to give you a representative sample of Spain's culinary wealth.

Whether you are a seasoned aficionado or a beginner in Spanish cuisine, we hope these recipes inspire you to explore new flavors and enjoy moments shared around the table with friends and family.

Olé!

table of Contents

Introduction	2
Paella	6
Tortilla Española	10
Gazpacho	13
Asturian Fabada	16
Galician -style octopus	20
Spanish Croquettes	24
Roman-style squid	28
ratatouille	31
Shrimp Scampi	34
Spicy potatoes	37
Salmorejo	41
Pintxos	44
Crumbs	46
Cod al Pil Pil	50
Valencian rice	53
Russian salad	57
Padrón Peppers	61
Meatballs in Spanish Sauce	64
Fideua	68
Porra Antequerana	72

	5
Roast pig	76
Seafood Cream	79
marmitako	83
Manchego ratatouille	87
Basque fish	91
Black Rice	94
Vizcaina style cod	98
Lobster stew	102
Mariscada	106
Desserts	110
Santiago's cake	111
Catalan cream	115
French toast	119
Donuts	123
Churros with chocolate	126

PAELLA

Preparation time: 1 hour
Servings: 4

Ingredients:

- 2 cups of bomb rice
- 4 cups chicken or seafood broth
- 300g chicken, cut into small pieces
- 200g rabbit, cut into small pieces (optional)
- 200g Spanish chorizo, sliced

- 200g shrimp
- 200g mussels
- 1 chopped onion
- 1 red pepper, cut into strips
- 1 green pepper, cut into strips
- 2 tomatoes, grated
- 3 cloves garlic, minced
- 1 teaspoon sweet paprika
- Saffron or food coloring, a pinch
- Salt and pepper to taste
- Olive oil

Preparation:

1. In a paella pan or large frying pan, heat a little olive oil over medium-high heat. Add the chicken and rabbit pieces (if using) and brown until cooked through. Remove from heat and reserve.

2. In the same paella pan, add a little more oil if necessary and fry the chorizo until lightly golden. Remove from the heat and set aside along with the chicken and rabbit.

3. In the same paella pan, add a little more oil if necessary and sauté the onion, peppers and garlic until tender.

4. Add the rice and sweet paprika, and stir well so that it is coated with the juices from the paella pan.

5. Pour the hot chicken or seafood broth into the paella pan. Add the saffron or food coloring and season with salt and pepper to taste. Stir gently to distribute the ingredients evenly.

6. Place the chicken, rabbit and chorizo pieces on top of the rice, distributing them evenly.

7. Add the grated tomatoes to the paella.

8. Cook over medium heat for about 15-20 minutes, or until the rice is cooked and the paella is golden brown on the bottom.

9. During the last few minutes of cooking, spread the shrimp and mussels over the paella and cook until the shrimp are pink and the mussels open.

10. Remove the paella from the heat and let it rest for a few minutes before serving.

11. Serve the paella hot, decorated with sliced lemon if you wish.

Enjoy your delicious Spanish paella!

TORTILLA ESPAÑOLA

Preparation time: 30 minutes
Servings: 4

Ingredients:

- 4-5 medium potatoes, peeled and cut into thin slices
- 1 large onion, cut into thin slices
- 6 large eggs
- Salt to taste

- Extra virgin olive oil

Preparation:

1. Heat plenty of olive oil in a large skillet over medium-high heat.

2. Add the potato slices to the pan and fry until golden and tender. Remove the potatoes from the pan and place them on absorbent paper to remove excess oil.

3. In the same pan, add the onion slices and cook until soft and slightly caramelized. Remove the onions from the pan and place them with the potatoes.

4. In a large bowl, beat the eggs and season with salt to taste.

5. Add the cooked potatoes and onions to the bowl with the beaten eggs and mix well so that all the ingredients are coated with egg.

6. Heat a little oil in a non-stick frying pan over medium heat.

7. Pour the egg, potato and onion mixture into the hot skillet and spread it evenly.

8. Cook the omelet for about 5-7 minutes or until the bottom is golden and set.

9. With the help of a plate or a lid, turn the tortilla to cook the other side. You can slide the omelet onto a large plate, then invert it back into the pan to cook the other side.

10. Cook the omelet for another 5-7 minutes or until completely cooked and golden brown on both sides.

11. Remove the tortilla from the heat and let it rest for a few minutes before cutting it into portions and serving.

12. Serve the Spanish tortilla hot or at room temperature, accompanied by a fresh salad and crusty bread.

Enjoy this classic and delicious Spanish tortilla!

GAZPACHO

Preparation time: 15 minutes
Servings: 4

Ingredients:

- 6 ripe tomatoes, cut into large pieces
- 1 large cucumber, peeled and coarsely cut
- 1 green bell pepper, cut into large pieces
- 1 clove garlic, peeled
- 1/4 red onion, cut into large pieces

- 2 tablespoons red wine vinegar
- 4 tablespoons extra virgin olive oil
- Salt to taste
- Freshly ground black pepper, to taste
- Ice cubes (optional, to serve)
- Chopped fresh parsley or basil leaves (optional, to decorate)

Preparation:

1. In a blender or food processor, add the tomatoes, cucumber, green pepper, garlic and red onion.
2. Add the red wine vinegar and extra virgin olive oil to the blender.
3. Salt and pepper to taste.
4. Blend all the ingredients until you obtain a smooth and homogeneous mixture.
5. Taste and adjust flavor with salt and pepper as needed.

6. Transfer the gazpacho to a large jar or container and refrigerate for at least 1 hour to cool and the flavors to blend.

7. Serve the cold gazpacho in individual bowls.

8. Optionally, you can add ice cubes to each bowl to keep it cold.

9. Garnish with fresh chopped parsley or basil leaves before serving, if desired.

Enjoy this refreshing and delicious gazpacho, perfect for hot summer days!

ASTURIAN Fabada

Preparation time: 12 hours (soaking the legumes) + 2 hours (cooking)
Servings: 4

Ingredients:

- 400g of fabes (Asturian white beans)
- 200g fresh bacon
- 2 Asturian chorizos
- 2 Asturian blood sausages

- 200g smoked pork or bacon
- 1 large onion, chopped
- 3 cloves garlic, minced
- 1 teaspoon sweet paprika
- Extra virgin olive oil
- Salt to taste

Preparation:

1. The night before cooking the fabada, soak the beans in plenty of cold water for at least 12 hours.

2. The next day, drain and rinse the soaked beans and place them in a large pot. Cover the beans with cold water and set the pot over medium-high heat.

3. When the water begins to boil, reduce the heat to low and cook the beans for about 2 hours, or until they are tender but not falling apart. During cooking, remove any

foam that forms on the surface with a slotted spoon.

4. While the beans are cooking, in a separate pan, heat a little olive oil and sauté the onion and garlic until golden and tender.

5. Add the sweet paprika to the sauce and cook for a couple more minutes, taking care not to burn it.

6. Add the sauce to the pot of cooked beans and stir well so that the flavors mix.

7. In another separate pot, cook the fresh bacon, chorizos, blood sausages and smoked bacon or bacon in boiling water for about 20-30 minutes to eliminate excess fat and pre-cook the meats.

8. Once cooked, add the meats to the pot of beans and cook everything together for about 20-30 more minutes over medium-low heat so that the flavors mix.

9. Taste the fabada and adjust the salt if necessary.

10. Serve the fabada hot in deep plates and accompany it with a piece of crusty bread.

Enjoy this delicious and comforting Asturian fabada, a traditional dish of Spanish gastronomy!

GALICIAN-STYLE OCTOPUS

Preparation time: 1 hour
Servings: 4

Ingredients:

- 1 octopus of approximately 1.5 kg
- 4-5 large potatoes
- Coarse salt
- Sweet paprika (La Vera paprika)
- Extra virgin olive oil

- Fine salt to taste
- Fresh parsley leaves (optional, to decorate)

Preparation:

1. Clean the octopus under cold water, removing any dirt or residue it may have. Cut off the end of the tentacles .

2. In a large pot, bring water to a boil. Add a pinch of coarse salt.

3. Submerge the octopus completely in the boiling water for a few seconds and remove it. Repeat this process three more times. This will help the octopus cook evenly and become more tender.

4. After the final blanching, place the octopus in the pot of boiling water and cook over medium heat for approximately 45-50 minutes, or until tender. To check cooking, prick the octopus with a

toothpick or knife; It should be tender and penetrate easily.

5. While the octopus is cooking, peel the potatoes and cut them into slices about 1cm thick.

6. In a separate pot, cook the potatoes in salted water until tender but firm. Drain them and reserve.

7. Once the octopus is cooked, remove it from the water and let it rest for a few minutes.

8. Cut the octopus into thick slices about 1cm thick.

9. On a large tray or plate, place the cooked potato slices.

10. On top of the potatoes, place the octopus slices.

11. Sprinkle generously with sweet paprika.

12. Drizzle everything with extra virgin olive oil.

13. Sprinkle with fine salt to taste.

14. Garnish with fresh parsley leaves if desired.

Enjoy this classic Galician dish, Galician-style octopus, accompanied by good crusty bread and a fresh white wine!

SPANISH CROQUETTES

Preparation time: 1 hour

Servings: 4

Ingredients:

- 100g butter
- 1 onion, finely chopped
- 100g Serrano or Iberian ham, chopped into small pieces
- 100g flour

- 500ml whole milk
- Salt and pepper to taste
- Nutmeg, to taste
- Bread crumbs
- 2 beaten eggs
- Oil for frying

Preparation:

1. In a large skillet, melt the butter over medium heat. Add the chopped onion and cook until translucent.
2. Add the chopped serrano ham to the pan and cook it along with the onion for a few minutes until golden and fragrant.
3. Add the flour to the pan and mix it well with the butter, onion and ham to form a thick paste.
4. Pour the hot milk little by little over the flour mixture, stirring constantly to avoid

lumps. Continue cooking and stirring until the sauce thickens and comes away easily from the sides of the pan.

5. Season the mixture with salt, pepper and nutmeg to taste. Remove the pan from the heat and let the mixture cool.

6. Once the mixture is cold and firm, form small croquettes with your hands, giving them the desired shape.

7. Dip the croquettes in breadcrumbs, then in beaten egg and again in breadcrumbs to coat them evenly.

8. Heat enough oil in a deep frying pan or deep fryer to 180°C.

9. Fry the croquettes in batches until golden brown and crispy on the outside.

10. Remove the croquettes from the hot oil and place them on absorbent paper to remove excess fat.

11. Serve the Spanish croquettes hot as an appetizer or as a side. Enjoy them!

I hope you enjoy these delicious Spanish croquettes!

ROMAN-STYLE SQUID

Preparation time: 30 minutes

Servings: 4

Ingredients:

- 500g squid, cleaned and cut into rings
- 100g wheat flour
- 2 beaten eggs
- Salt to taste
- Black pepper to taste

- Vegetable oil for frying
- Lemon (optional, to serve)
- Chopped fresh parsley (optional, to decorate)

Preparation:

1. In a bowl, mix the flour with salt and pepper to taste.
2. Dredge the squid rings in the flour, making sure to coat them completely.
3. Gently shake the squid rings to remove excess flour.
4. Dip the floured squid rings into the beaten egg, making sure they are well coated.
5. Heat plenty of vegetable oil in a deep skillet or deep fryer over medium-high heat.
6. When the oil is hot, fry the squid rings in batches until golden and crispy, about 2-3 minutes per side.

7. Remove the fried squid from the hot oil and place on absorbent paper to remove excess fat.

8. Repeat the process with the rest of the squid rings.

9. Once all the calamari is fried, serve it hot as an appetizer or main dish.

10. Optionally, you can serve the Roman-style squid with lemon slices and sprinkle fresh chopped parsley on top to give it a touch of freshness and color.

Enjoy these delicious Roman-style squid as part of your lunch or dinner!

PISTO (SPANISH RATATOUILLE)

Preparation time: 45 minutes
Servings: 4

Ingredients:

- 4 ripe tomatoes
- 2 green peppers
- 2 medium zucchini
- 1 large onion

- 2 cloves of garlic
- 2 tablespoons olive oil
- Salt to taste
- Black pepper to taste
- Optional: fried egg (to accompany)

Preparation:

1. Cut the tomatoes into small pieces. Finely chop the onion and garlic cloves. Cut the green peppers and zucchini into small cubes.

2. In a large skillet, heat the olive oil over medium heat. Add the onion and chopped garlic cloves and cook until golden and fragrant.

3. Add the chopped green peppers to the pan and cook for a few minutes until tender.

4. Add the cut zucchini to the pan and cook for a few more minutes until lightly golden.

5. Add the chopped tomatoes to the pan and mix well with the rest of the vegetables. Cook over medium-low heat for about 20-25 minutes, stirring occasionally, until the vegetables are tender and a thick sauce has formed.

6. Season the ratatouille with salt and pepper to taste.

7. Once the ratatouille is ready, remove the pan from the heat and serve hot.

8. Optionally, you can accompany the ratatouille with a fried egg on top of each portion.

Enjoy this delicious ratatouille, perfect as a main dish or as a side dish!

SHRIMP SCAMPI

Preparation time: 15 minutes

Servings: 4

Ingredients:

- 500g raw shrimp, peeled and deveined
- 6 cloves garlic, finely chopped
- 1 chilli (optional), finely chopped

- 1/4 cup extra virgin olive oil
- 1 tablespoon chopped fresh parsley
- Salt to taste
- Bread to accompany

Preparation:

1. Heat the olive oil in a large skillet over medium heat.
2. Add the chopped garlic and chilli (if using) to the pan and cook for a few minutes until the garlic begins to lightly brown and release its aroma.
3. Add the peeled prawns to the pan and cook for about 2-3 minutes, stirring occasionally, until pink and cooked through.
4. Season the garlic shrimp with salt to taste and sprinkle the chopped fresh parsley on top. Stir well to make sure the shrimp are well coated with the garlic and parsley.

5. Remove the pan from the heat and serve the garlic shrimp hot, accompanied by crusty bread to dip in the delicious garlic oil.

Enjoy these delicious garlic shrimp as an appetizer or as part of a traditional Spanish meal!

SPICY POTATOES

Preparation time: 45 minutes

Servings: 4

Ingredients:

- 4 medium potatoes
- 2 tablespoons olive oil
- 1 teaspoon sweet paprika
- 1/2 teaspoon hot paprika (optional)
- Salt to taste

- Brava sauce (see recipe below)
- Aioli (see recipe below)
- Chopped fresh parsley (optional, to decorate)

Preparation:

1. Preheat the oven to 200°C (390°F).
2. Wash and peel the potatoes, then cut them into cubes approximately 2 cm on a side.
3. Place the potatoes on a baking sheet and toss with the olive oil, sweet paprika, hot paprika (if using) and salt to taste, making sure they are well coated.
4. Bake the potatoes in the preheated oven for about 30-35 minutes, or until tender on the inside and crispy on the outside, stirring occasionally so they cook evenly.
5. Meanwhile, prepare the brava sauce and aioli (see recipes below).

6. Once the potatoes are ready, remove them from the oven and serve them hot, accompanied by salsa brava and aioli. Sprinkle fresh chopped parsley on top, if desired, for a touch of freshness and color.

Brave sauce:

- 4 tablespoons olive oil
- 2 cloves garlic, finely chopped
- 1 teaspoon hot paprika
- 1 teaspoon sweet paprika
- 1 tablespoon of flour
- 1/2 cup vegetable broth or water
- Salt to taste

1. In a frying pan, heat the olive oil over medium heat. Add the minced garlic and cook until golden and fragrant.
2. Add the hot paprika and sweet paprika to the pan and cook for another minute.

3. Add the flour to the pan and cook, stirring constantly, for a few minutes so that it cooks and does not taste raw.

4. Pour the vegetable broth or water into the pan, little by little, while stirring to avoid lumps. Cook the sauce until thickened, season with salt to taste, and remove from heat.

Aioli :

- 1/2 cup mayonnaise
- 1 clove garlic, finely chopped
- Juice of 1/2 lemon
- Salt to taste

1. In a small bowl, mix the mayonnaise, minced garlic and lemon juice.
2. Season with salt to taste and mix well.

I hope you enjoy these delicious patatas bravas!

SALMOREJO

Preparation time: 15 minutes

Servings: 4

Ingredients:

- 1 kg of ripe tomatoes
- 200 g stale bread (preferably loaf)
- 1 clove garlic
- 100 ml extra virgin olive oil
- 30 ml sherry vinegar

- Salt to taste
- Hard-boiled eggs and chopped serrano ham to decorate (optional)

Preparation:

1. Soak stale bread in water for a few minutes to soften it. Drain and squeeze to remove excess water.
2. Wash the tomatoes and cut them into large pieces. Peel the garlic clove.
3. In the glass of a blender, place the chopped tomatoes, the soaked and drained bread, the garlic clove, the extra virgin olive oil, the sherry vinegar and a pinch of salt.
4. Blend all the ingredients until you obtain a smooth and homogeneous cream.
5. Taste the salmorejo and adjust the salt and vinegar according to your personal taste.

6. Refrigerate the salmorejo for at least 1 hour before serving so that it is very cold.

7. Serve the salmorejo in individual bowls and decorate with chopped hard-boiled egg and serrano ham if you wish. You can also drizzle a little extra virgin olive oil before serving.

Enjoy this delicious and refreshing typical Spanish dish!

PINTXOS

Preparation time: Variable
Portions: Variable

Ingredients:

- Bread (baguette or similar)
- Ingredients for toppings (they can be varied, such as serrano ham, cheese, olives, anchovies, roasted peppers, etc.)
- Chopsticks or small skewers

Preparation:

1. Cut the bread into thin slices and toast them lightly in a toaster or in the oven.
2. Prepare the ingredients for the toppings according to your preferences. You can cut the ham into small pieces, cut the cheese into wedges, pit the olives, etc.
3. Place the ingredients on the toasted bread slices, combining them according to your taste.
4. Skewer the pintxos with toothpicks or small skewers to keep the ingredients in place.
5. Serve the pintxos on a tray and ready to enjoy!

Note: Pintxos are very versatile, so feel free to experiment with different ingredient combinations and presentations to create your own unique versions. Enjoy them!

CRUMBS

Preparation time: 45 minutes

Servings: 4

Ingredients:

- 400 g day-old bread (preferably loaf)
- 150 ml extra virgin olive oil
- 4 cloves of garlic
- 150 g of bacon or chorizo (optional)

- 1 green pepper
- 1 red pepper
- 1 large onion
- Salt to taste
- Sweet paprika (optional)
- Water

Preparation:

1. Cut the bread into small pieces and let it air for a few hours or overnight to harden.
2. In a large skillet, heat the extra virgin olive oil over medium heat.
3. Peel and finely chop the garlic cloves and add them to the hot oil. Cook the garlic until golden and fragrant.
4. If you are using pancetta or chorizo, cut them into small pieces and add them to the pan. Cook until golden and crispy.

5. Cut the peppers and onion into small pieces and add them to the pan. Cook the vegetables until tender.

6. Add the stale bread to the sautéed vegetables and mix well. If you wish, you can sprinkle a little paprika over the crumbs for additional color and flavor.

7. Add a little water to the crumbs to help them moisten and cook evenly. Gradually add water as needed until the crumbs are tender but not too wet.

8. Cook the crumbs over medium-low heat, stirring occasionally, until cooked through and golden brown all over.

9. Taste the crumbs and adjust the salt if necessary.

10. Serve the migas hot accompanied by grapes, melon or any other fresh fruit, and enjoy this delicious traditional Spanish dish!

I hope you enjoy these delicious crumbs!

COD AL PIL PIL

Preparation time: 30 minutes

Servings: 4

Ingredients:

- 4 loins of desalted cod (approximately 150 g each)
- 4 cloves of garlic
- 200 ml extra virgin olive oil
- Chilli (optional)

- Salt

Preparation:

1. Dry the cod loins well with kitchen paper to remove excess moisture.

2. Heat the extra virgin olive oil in a large skillet over medium heat.

3. Add the whole, unpeeled garlic cloves to the pan. You can also add a whole chilli if you prefer a spicy touch to the dish.

4. When the garlic starts to brown slightly, add the cod fillets to the pan, skin side down.

5. Cook the cod over medium-low heat for about 8-10 minutes, gently shaking the pan occasionally to prevent sticking. It is important not to turn the cod during cooking.

6. As the cod cooks, the juices from the garlic and oil will emulsify forming a

delicious pil sauce. pil . If the sauce is not thick enough, you can help emulsify it by gently moving the pan or shaking it from side to side.

7. When the cod is cooked and the sauce has a creamy, glossy texture, remove the pan from the heat.

8. Remove the garlic and chilli from the pan and adjust the salt to taste.

9. Serve the cod al pil hot pil , accompanied by some slices of bread to dip in the delicious sauce.

I hope you enjoy this classic Basque dish!

VALENCIAN RICE

Preparation time: 1 hour

Servings: 4

Ingredients:

- 300 g bomb rice
- 500 g chicken (thighs or breasts) cut into pieces

- 300 g chopped rabbit (optional)
- 200 g green beans
- 1 grated ripe tomato
- 1 red pepper cut into strips
- 1 green pepper cut into strips
- 1 chopped onion
- 2 cloves of garlic, minced
- 1 teaspoon sweet paprika
- Saffron or food coloring
- Salt to taste
- Extra virgin olive oil
- Hot chicken or vegetable broth (double the volume of rice)

Preparation:

1. In a paella pan or large saucepan, heat a little extra virgin olive oil over medium-high heat.

2. Add the chopped chicken and rabbit and sauté until golden brown on all sides. Remove the meat from the paella pan and reserve.

3. In the same paella pan, add a little more oil if necessary and sauté the chopped onion, peppers and garlic until tender.

4. Add the grated tomato and cook for a few minutes until it has reduced and thickened slightly.

5. Add the green beans cut into pieces and cook for a few more minutes.

6. Add the sweet paprika and mix well.

7. Add the rice and stir to coat it with all the flavors.

8. Pour the hot broth into the paella pan, making sure it lightly covers the rice. Add a

pinch of saffron or food coloring and salt to taste.

9. Cook over medium-high heat for about 10 minutes and then reduce the heat to medium-low and continue cooking for another 10-15 minutes, or until the rice is tender and has absorbed all the liquid.

10. Once the rice is ready, add the reserved chicken and rabbit and mix well.

11. Remove the paella pan from the heat and let it rest for a few minutes before serving.

12. Serve the Valencian Rice hot and enjoy this classic Spanish dish!

I hope this recipe is useful to you and that you enjoy preparing and tasting this delicious Valencian Rice. Enjoy!

RUSSIAN SALAD

Preparation time: 30 minutes

Servings: 4

Ingredients:

- 4 medium potatoes
- 2 medium carrots
- 150 g peas (can be fresh or canned)
- 4 eggs
- 100 g green beans (optional)

- 4-5 tablespoons mayonnaise
- Salt to taste
- Ground black pepper (optional)
- Chopped fresh parsley (optional, to decorate)

Preparation:

1. Cook potatoes and carrots in a large pot of salted water until tender but firm. This will take around 20-25 minutes. Then, remove them from the water and let them cool.

2. In another pot, cook the eggs in boiling water for about 10 minutes. Once cooked, cool them under cold water and peel them.

3. If you are using green beans, cut them into small pieces and cook them in salted water until crisp-tender. Then drain and cool them.

4. Cut the potatoes, carrots and eggs into small pieces and put them in a large bowl.

5. Add the peas and green beans (if using) to the bowl with the potatoes, carrots and eggs.

6. Add the mayonnaise to the bowl and gently mix all the ingredients until well combined. If you wish, you can add a little salt and ground black pepper to season to taste.

7. Taste the salad and adjust the amount of mayonnaise and seasoning as needed.

8. Cover the bowl with plastic wrap and refrigerate the salad for at least 1 hour before serving, so the flavors blend well and the salad is fresh and delicious.

9. Before serving, you can garnish the salad with chopped fresh parsley for an extra touch of color and flavor.

Enjoy your Russian Salad as a delicious side or main dish!

PADRÓN PEPPERS

Preparation time: 15 minutes
Servings: 4

Ingredients:

- 250 g Padrón peppers
- Extra virgin olive oil
- Coarse salt

Preparation:

1. Wash the Padrón peppers under cold water and dry them well with kitchen paper.

2. Heat a large skillet over medium-high heat. Add a generous splash of extra virgin olive oil and let it heat up.

3. When the oil is hot, add the Padrón peppers to the pan. Spread them in a single layer so they cook evenly.

4. Cook the peppers for 5-7 minutes, stirring occasionally with a spatula, until tender and lightly browned in places.

5. Once cooked, remove the peppers from the pan and drain them on kitchen paper to remove excess oil.

6. Transfer the Padrón peppers to a serving plate and sprinkle with coarse salt to taste.

7. Serve the Padrón peppers immediately as an appetizer or side. And remember, "some pepper is hot"!

Ready! Enjoy these delicious Padrón Peppers as an easy and delicious appetizer.

MEATBALLS IN SPANISH SAUCE

Preparation time: 30 minutes

Servings: 4

Ingredients:

For the meatballs:

- 500 g minced meat (beef, pork or mix)
- 1 egg
- 1/2 cup breadcrumbs

- 1 clove garlic, finely chopped
- 1/4 cup fresh parsley, chopped
- Salt and pepper to taste
- Olive oil for frying

For the Spanish sauce:

- 1 onion, finely chopped
- 2 cloves garlic, finely chopped
- 2 carrots, peeled and cut into thin slices
- 2 tablespoons of flour
- 2 cups of meat broth
- 1 can of crushed tomato (400 g)
- 1 bay leaf
- Salt and pepper to taste

Preparation:

1. In a large bowl, mix the minced meat with the egg, breadcrumbs, minced garlic,

chopped parsley, salt and pepper. Knead the mixture until well combined.

2. Form meatballs of the desired size with the meat mixture and set aside.

3. Heat some olive oil in a large skillet over medium-high heat. Fry the meatballs until golden brown on all sides. Remove them from the pan and set aside.

4. In the same pan, add a little more oil if necessary and cook the onion, garlic and carrots until tender.

5. Sprinkle the flour over the vegetables and cook for a couple of minutes.

6. Pour the meat broth and crushed tomato into the pan. Add the bay leaf and season with salt and pepper to taste. Let the sauce come to a boil and then reduce the heat to medium-low.

7. Place the meatballs in the sauce and simmer for about 15-20 minutes, or until

the meatballs are cooked through and the sauce has thickened.

8. Remove the bay leaf and serve the meatballs hot accompanied by the Spanish sauce. You can serve them with chips, rice or bread to dip in the sauce.

Enjoy these delicious Meatballs in Spanish Sauce, a comforting dish full of flavor!

FIDEUA

Preparation time: 40 minutes

Servings: 4

Ingredients:

- 250 g thick noodles for fideuà
- 300 g of shrimp
- 300 g squid, cleaned and cut into rings
- 1 chopped onion
- 2 cloves garlic, minced

- 1 red pepper, cut into thin strips
- 2 ripe tomatoes, grated
- 1 liter of fish broth
- 1 teaspoon sweet paprika
- Saffron or food coloring
- Extra virgin olive oil
- Salt to taste
- Lemon (optional)
- Chopped fresh parsley (optional)

Preparation:

1. In a large paella pan or frying pan, heat a little olive oil over medium-high heat. Sauté the prawns and squid for a few minutes until golden brown. Remove and reserve.

2. In the same paella pan, add a little more oil if necessary and sauté the onion, garlic and red pepper until tender.

3. Add the grated tomatoes and sweet paprika. Cook for a few minutes until the tomatoes have reduced and the mixture is well integrated.

4. Add the noodles to the paella pan and mix them with the sauce. Lightly toast the noodles for a few minutes.

5. Pour the hot fish broth over the noodles and add a pinch of saffron or food coloring. Cook over medium heat for about 10-12 minutes, stirring occasionally, until the noodles are al dente and the liquid has been absorbed.

6. When the noodles are almost ready, place the shrimp and squid back on the fideuà to warm up.

7. Adjust the seasoning with salt to taste and remove from heat.

8. Serve the fideuà hot, decorated with lemon slices and sprinkled with fresh chopped parsley if you wish.

Enjoy this delicious Fideuà , a classic dish of Mediterranean cuisine with all the flavor of the sea!

PORRA ANTEQUERANA

Preparation time: 15 minutes

Servings: 4

Ingredients:

- 500 g ripe tomatoes
- 1 green pepper
- 1 cucumber

- 2 cloves of garlic
- 100 g stale bread
- 50 ml extra virgin olive oil
- 20 ml wine vinegar
- Salt to taste
- Hard-boiled eggs (optional, to decorate)
- Chopped serrano ham (optional, to decorate)
- Roasted peppers (optional, to decorate)

Preparation:

1. Soak stale bread in water for a few minutes to soften it.
2. Meanwhile, wash and cut the tomatoes, green pepper and cucumber into large pieces.
3. In a blender or food processor, add the tomatoes, green pepper, cucumber,

peeled garlic cloves, and soaked and drained bread.

4. Add the extra virgin olive oil and wine vinegar to the mixture in the blender.

5. Blend everything at maximum power until you obtain a smooth and homogeneous cream. If necessary, add a little water to obtain the desired consistency.

6. Taste the antequerana porra and adjust the seasoning with salt to taste.

7. Refrigerate the porra for at least 1 hour before serving so that it is very cold.

8. Serve the Porra Antequerana in individual bowls and decorate with chopped hard-boiled egg, chopped serrano ham and roasted peppers if desired.

9. Accompany the porra with some fried bread croutons or some olives to enjoy an authentic Andalusian flavor.

I hope you enjoy this refreshing and delicious Porra Antequerana, perfect for hot summer days!

ROAST PIG

Preparation time: 30 minutes

Servings: 4

Ingredients:

- 1 whole suckling pig (approximately 4-5 kg)
- Coarse salt
- Extra virgin olive oil
- Ground black pepper

- Fresh rosemary (optional, for flavoring)

Preparation:

1. Preheat the oven to 200°C (390°F).

2. Wash the suckling pig inside and out, and dry it completely with kitchen paper.

3. Make a few cuts in the skin of the suckling pig with a sharp knife to help it brown and crisp up during cooking.

4. Rub the skin of the suckling pig with olive oil and season generously with coarse salt and ground black pepper. You can place a few sprigs of fresh rosemary inside the suckling pig to give it aroma if you wish.

5. Place the suckling pig on a baking tray with the skin side up.

6. Bake the suckling pig in the preheated oven for about 2 hours, or until the skin is golden and crispy and the meat is tender and cooked through. During cooking, you

can water the suckling pig with its own juices to keep it juicy.

7. Once cooked, remove the suckling pig from the oven and let it rest for a few minutes before cutting it into individual portions.

8. Serve the roast suckling pig hot accompanied by traditional garnishes such as roast potatoes, roast vegetables or salad.

Enjoy this delicious and classic Spanish roast suckling pig dish!

SEAFOOD CREAM

Preparation time: 45 minutes

Servings: 4

Ingredients:

- 500 g of various seafood (prawns, prawns, mussels, clams, etc.)
- 1 large onion, finely chopped
- 2 cloves garlic, finely chopped
- 2 carrots, peeled and diced
- 2 stalks celery, diced

- 1 leek, sliced
- 2 ripe tomatoes, peeled and chopped
- 1 liter of fish broth
- 200 ml cooking cream
- 50 ml brandy or white wine (optional)
- 2 tablespoons extra virgin olive oil
- Salt and pepper to taste
- Chopped fresh parsley, to decorate

Preparation:

1. In a large pot, heat the olive oil over medium heat. Add the onion, garlic, carrots, celery and leek, and cook until tender, about 5-7 minutes.
2. Add the chopped tomatoes and cook for a few more minutes.

3. Add the seafood (previously cleaned and shelled, if necessary) to the pot and sauté for a few minutes until cooked.

4. Pour the fish broth into the pot and let the mixture boil. Reduce the heat and simmer for about 15-20 minutes so the flavors blend well.

5. If you are using brandy or white wine, add it to the pot and let it cook for a couple of minutes to allow the alcohol to evaporate.

6. Remove the pot from the heat and use a hand blender to blend the mixture until you obtain a smooth cream.

7. Place the pot back on the heat and add the cooking cream. Simmer for a few more minutes, stirring occasionally, until the cream is hot.

8. Taste the cream and adjust the seasoning with salt and pepper to taste.

9. Serve the seafood cream hot, sprinkled with fresh chopped parsley to decorate.

Enjoy this delicious seafood cream as a starter or main course at a special meal!

MARMITAKO

Preparation time: 1 hour

Servings: 4

Ingredients:

- 600 g fresh tuna, cut into cubes
- 4 medium potatoes, peeled and cut into large pieces
- 1 large onion, chopped
- 2 green peppers, cut into strips

- 2 ripe tomatoes, peeled and chopped
- 2 cloves garlic, minced
- 1 chorizo pepper, hydrated and seeded
- 1 pinch of sweet paprika
- 1 bay leaf
- Extra virgin olive oil
- Salt to taste
- Water
- Chopped fresh parsley, to decorate

Preparation:

1. In a large pot, heat some olive oil over medium heat. Add the onion and green peppers and sauté until tender.
2. Add the chopped tomatoes and minced garlic cloves to the pot. Cook for a few more minutes until the tomatoes have

broken down and the mixture is cooked through.

3. Add the potatoes cut into large pieces to the pot and mix well with the sauce.

4. Add enough water to cover the potatoes and bring the mixture to a boil.

5. Once it boils, add the hydrated and seeded chorizo pepper, the bay leaf and a pinch of sweet paprika. Mix well.

6. Reduce the heat to medium-low and cook the mixture for about 20 minutes, or until the potatoes are almost tender.

7. Add the bonito cubes to the pot and cook for another 10-15 minutes, or until the bonito is cooked but still juicy.

8. Taste and adjust seasoning with salt to taste.

9. Remove the pot from the heat and let the marmitako rest for a few minutes before serving.

10. Serve hot, sprinkled with fresh chopped parsley to decorate.

Enjoy this delicious traditional Basque marmitako dish!

MANCHEGO PISTO (SPANISH RATATOUILLE)

Preparation time: 45 minutes
Servings: 4

Ingredients:

- 2 medium eggplants, cut into cubes
- 2 medium zucchini, cut into cubes
- 2 red peppers, cut into cubes

- 2 green peppers, cut into cubes
- 1 large onion, chopped
- 4 ripe tomatoes, peeled and chopped
- 4 cloves garlic, minced
- 1/4 cup extra virgin olive oil
- Salt to taste
- Ground black pepper to taste
- 1 teaspoon sugar (optional)
- Chopped fresh parsley to decorate (optional)

Preparation:

1. In a large skillet, heat the olive oil over medium heat. Add the chopped garlic and sauté until golden and fragrant.
2. Add the chopped onion to the pan and cook until translucent.

3. Add the red and green peppers to the pan and cook until tender.

4. Add the chopped tomatoes to the pan and cook the mixture until the tomatoes have broken down and the mixture has a thicker consistency.

5. Add the eggplant and zucchini to the pan and cook until tender but still holding their shape. If necessary, you can add a little water to help cook the vegetables.

6. If the ratatouille is too sour due to the tomatoes, you can add a teaspoon of sugar to balance the flavors.

7. Season the ratatouille with salt and pepper to taste and cook for a few more minutes.

8. Remove the pan from the heat and let the ratatouille rest for a few minutes before serving.

9. Serve the Manchego ratatouille hot, sprinkled with fresh chopped parsley if desired.

Enjoy this delicious and traditional Spanish pisto manchego recipe!

BASQUE FISH

Preparation time: 45 minutes

Servings: 4

Ingredients:

- 4 white fish fillets (hake, cod, sea bass, etc.), approximately 150-200 g each
- 2 ripe tomatoes, peeled and chopped
- 1 large onion, finely chopped
- 2 cloves garlic, finely chopped
- 1 green pepper, cut into strips

- 1 red pepper, cut into strips
- 1 yellow bell pepper, cut into strips
- 100 ml white wine
- 100 ml fish broth
- 2 tablespoons extra virgin olive oil
- Salt and pepper to taste
- Chopped fresh parsley, to decorate

Preparation:

1. In a large skillet or saucepan, heat the olive oil over medium heat. Add the onion and garlic, and cook until golden and tender.
2. Add the sliced peppers to the pan and sauté for a few minutes until tender.
3. Add the chopped tomatoes to the pan and cook for a few more minutes, until they reduce and thicken slightly.

4. Pour the white wine and fish stock into the pan. Bring to a boil and then reduce heat to medium-low. Let the sauce simmer for about 10-15 minutes to allow the flavors to blend.

5. Meanwhile, season the fish fillets with salt and pepper to taste.

6. When the sauce is ready, place the fish fillets in the pan, making sure they are well covered by the sauce. Cover the pan and cook over low heat for about 10-15 minutes, or until the fish is cooked and flakes easily with a fork.

7. Once the fish is cooked, remove the pan from the heat. Sprinkle fresh chopped parsley on top as decoration.

8. Serve the Basque Fish hot , accompanied by crusty bread or white rice if you wish.

Enjoy this delicious recipe from Basque cuisine!

BLACK RICE

Preparation time: 40 minutes

Servings: 4

Ingredients:

- 300 g bomb rice (you can also use brown rice)

- 500 g squid, cleaned and cut into rings
- 1 large onion, finely chopped
- 4 cloves garlic, minced
- 1 red bell pepper, cut into small pieces
- 1 ripe tomato, grated
- 1 liter of fish broth or vegetable broth
- 150 ml dry white wine
- 1 teaspoon sweet paprika
- 1 teaspoon hot paprika (optional)
- 1 sachet of squid ink (approximately 4 g)
- Salt to taste
- Extra virgin olive oil

Preparation:

1. In a paella pan or large frying pan, heat a little olive oil over medium-high heat. Add the squid and brown them lightly for a few

minutes. Remove them from the pan and set aside.

2. In the same pan, add a little more oil if necessary. Add the onion, garlic and red pepper, and cook until tender and translucent.

3. Add the grated tomato to the pan and cook for a few minutes until reduced and thickened slightly.

4. Add the rice to the pan and mix well with the sautéed vegetables. Cook for a couple of minutes, stirring constantly.

5. Pour the white wine into the pan and stir until the alcohol evaporates.

6. Dilute the squid ink in a little hot broth and add it to the pan along with the rest of the fish broth. Also add sweet paprika and, if you prefer, hot paprika. Adjust salt to taste.

7. Cook the rice over medium heat for about 20-25 minutes, or until it is tender and has

absorbed most of the liquid. Do not stir the rice while it is cooking to prevent it from breaking.

8. When the rice is ready, turn off the heat and let it rest for a few minutes before serving.

9. Serve the Black Rice hot, decorated with the golden squid rings that you reserved previously.

I hope you enjoy this delicious black rice dish!

VIZCAINA STYLE COD

Preparation time: 1 hour

Servings: 4

Ingredients:

- 4 loins of desalted cod
- 4 ripe tomatoes
- 1 large onion
- 2 cloves of garlic
- 1 red pepper

- 50 g almonds
- 50 g pitted green olives
- 1 bay leaf
- 1/2 glass of white wine
- Extra virgin olive oil
- Salt and pepper to taste

Preparation:

1. Preheat the oven to 180ºC (350ºF).
2. On a baking sheet, place the tomatoes, onion and pepper cut into large pieces. Add the whole, unpeeled garlic cloves. Drizzle with a little olive oil, season with salt and bake for about 30-40 minutes or until the vegetables are tender and lightly browned.
3. Meanwhile, toast the almonds in a skillet over medium heat until lightly golden. Booking.

4. When the vegetables are ready, remove from the oven and let cool slightly. Peel the roasted garlic cloves.

5. In a large frying pan, heat a little olive oil and sauté the bay leaf for a few minutes. Add the roasted vegetables, roasted garlic cloves, toasted almonds and green olives. Cook everything together for about 5 minutes.

6. Remove the bay leaf and blend the mixture with a blender until you obtain a homogeneous sauce. If necessary, add a little water to obtain the desired consistency.

7. In the same pan, heat a little more oil and add the cod loins. Cook over medium-high heat for about 3-4 minutes on each side, or until golden brown.

8. Pour the Vizcaya sauce over the cod and cook over medium-low heat for about 5 more minutes, or until the cod is

completely cooked and the sauce has heated through.

9. Serve the Biscayan-style cod hot, accompanied by a good piece of bread to dip in the delicious sauce.

Enjoy this exquisite recipe for Biscayan cod, a traditional dish of Basque cuisine!

LOBSTER STEW

Preparation time: 1 hour

Servings: 4

Ingredients:

- 2 medium lobsters
- 2 ripe tomatoes
- 1 large onion
- 2 cloves of garlic
- 1 red pepper

- 1 green pepper
- 1 carrot
- 1/2 glass of brandy
- 1/2 glass of white wine
- 1 liter of fish broth
- Extra virgin olive oil
- Salt and pepper to taste
- Chopped fresh parsley, to decorate

Preparation:

1. Preheat the oven to 180°C (350°F).
2. Split the lobsters in half lengthwise with a sharp knife. Wash the heads and tails of the lobsters well. Booking.
3. On a baking sheet, place the tomatoes, onion, garlic cloves, peppers and carrot cut into large pieces. Drizzle with a little olive oil, season with salt and bake for

about 30-40 minutes or until the vegetables are tender and lightly browned.

4. Meanwhile, in a large skillet, heat some olive oil over medium-high heat. Add the lobsters and brown them on both sides for about 5 minutes. Remove the lobsters from the pan and set aside.

5. In the same pan, pour the brandy and white wine. Bring to a boil and scrape up any browned bits stuck to the bottom of the pan to mix with the liquid.

6. Add the roasted vegetables to the pan and cook for a few more minutes, mashing the vegetables with a wooden spoon to make a thick paste.

7. Pour the fish broth into the pan and let it boil. Reduce heat and simmer for about 20 minutes, stirring occasionally.

8. When the sauce has reduced slightly, place the lobsters in the pan. Simmer for another 10 minutes, or until the lobsters are cooked through and the sauce has thickened.

9. Serve the lobster stew hot, sprinkled with fresh chopped parsley to decorate.

Enjoy this delicious lobster stew, a typical dish of Mediterranean cuisine with a touch of luxury!

MARISCADA

Preparation time: 45 minutes
Servings: 4

Ingredients:

- 500g prawns
- 500g mussels
- 500g clams

- 500g squid, cleaned and cut into rings
- 500g shrimp
- 4 cloves garlic, minced
- 1 large onion, chopped
- 2 ripe tomatoes, chopped
- 1 red pepper, chopped
- 1 green pepper, chopped
- 1 glass of white wine
- 1/2 cup fish broth
- Extra virgin olive oil
- Salt and pepper to taste
- Chopped fresh parsley, to decorate
- Lemon, sliced (optional)

Preparation:

1. Wash the mussels and clams well under cold running water to remove any sand

residue. Discard any mussels and clams that are open or cracked.

2. In a large saucepan, heat a little olive oil over medium heat. Add the prawns and shrimp, and sauté until pink and cooked on both sides. Remove from heat and reserve.

3. In the same saucepan, add a little more olive oil if necessary. Add the minced garlic and onion, and cook until golden and fragrant.

4. Add the chopped red and green peppers, and tomatoes. Cook until the peppers are tender and the tomatoes have broken down.

5. Add the squid cut into rings and cook for a few more minutes.

6. Pour the white wine into the saucepan and let it boil over high heat so that the alcohol evaporates.

7. Add the fish stock and bring the mixture to a boil.

8. Add the mussels and clams to the casserole. Cover with a lid and cook until the mussels and clams open, about 5 minutes. Discard any that do not open.

9. Return the prawns and shrimp to the pot and heat for a few more minutes.

10. Adjust the seasoning with salt and pepper to taste.

11. Serve the seafood platter hot, sprinkled with fresh chopped parsley and accompanied with lemon slices if you wish.

Enjoy this delicious seafood platter, full of fresh flavors from the sea!

Desserts

SANTIAGO'S CAKE

Preparation time: 1 hour

Servings: 8

Ingredients:

For the mass:

- 200 g ground almonds
- 200g sugar
- 4 eggs
- Zest of 1 lemon

- 1 teaspoon ground cinnamon
- Butter or oil to grease the mold
- Flour to sprinkle

For decoration (optional):

- Powdered sugar
- Stencil of the Cross of Santiago

Preparation:

1. Preheat the oven to 180°C (350°F). Grease a round mold of approximately 22 cm in diameter with butter or oil and sprinkle with flour to prevent the cake from sticking.
2. In a large bowl, beat the eggs with the sugar until the mixture is foamy and has doubled in volume.
3. Add the lemon zest and ground cinnamon to the egg and sugar mixture, and mix well.

4. Add the ground almonds to the mixture, little by little, until they are completely integrated and you obtain a homogeneous dough.

5. Pour the batter into the prepared pan and spread it evenly with a spatula.

6. Bake the cake in the preheated oven for approximately 35-40 minutes, or until golden brown on the top and a toothpick inserted into the center comes out clean.

7. Remove the cake from the oven and let it cool in the pan for a few minutes before removing it from the pan. Then let it cool completely on a rack.

8. If you wish, you can decorate the Santiago Cake with icing sugar sprinkled on top and placing a stencil of the Cross of Santiago on it to give it a traditional touch.

9. Serve the Tarta de Santiago in generous portions and enjoy this delicious traditional Spanish dessert!

I hope you enjoy this delicious Tarta de Santiago, a classic dessert of Spanish gastronomy!

CATALAN CREAM

Preparation time: 30 minutes

Servings: 4

Ingredients:

- 4 egg yolks
- 500 ml whole milk
- 100g sugar

- 1 cinnamon stick
- The peel of 1 lemon
- 30 g cornstarch
- Sugar to caramelize the surface

Preparation:

1. In a bowl, mix the egg yolks with the sugar until you obtain a homogeneous and creamy mixture. Add the cornstarch and mix well.
2. In a saucepan, heat the milk along with the cinnamon stick and lemon peel until it is about to boil.
3. Remove the cinnamon and lemon peel from the hot milk.
4. Slowly pour the hot milk over the egg yolk, sugar and cornstarch mixture, stirring constantly to prevent the yolks from curdling.

5. Pour the mixture back into the saucepan and heat over medium-low heat, stirring constantly with a wooden spoon, until the cream thickens and coats the back of the spoon. This will take about 5-10 minutes.

6. Remove the cream from the heat and pour it into individual containers or a large mold.

7. Let the cream cool to room temperature and then refrigerate it for at least 2 hours, or until very cold.

8. Just before serving, sprinkle a thin layer of sugar over the surface of each serving of cream.

9. Caramelize the sugar with a kitchen torch or by placing the containers under the grill of the preheated oven for a few minutes, until the sugar melts and forms a golden, crispy layer.

10. Serve the crème brûlée immediately, enjoying the contrast between the creaminess of the cream and the crunchy caramel layer.

I hope you enjoy this delicious Crema Catalana, a classic dessert from Spanish cuisine!

FRENCH TOAST

Preparation time: 30 minutes

Servings: 4

Ingredients:

- 1 loaf of bread from the previous day (preferably with a dense crumb, like village bread)
- 500 ml of milk
- 100g sugar

- 1 cinnamon stick
- The peel of 1 lemon (without the white part)
- 3 eggs
- Mild olive oil for frying
- Sugar and cinnamon to sprinkle

Preparation:

1. In a saucepan, heat the milk along with the sugar, cinnamon stick and lemon peel over medium heat. Stir until the sugar is completely dissolved and then let it cool.
2. Meanwhile, cut the bread into slices about 2cm thick.
3. Place the bread slices on a large tray and pour the warm milk over them. Let the bread soak for at least 15-20 minutes, turning it halfway through to make sure it soaks well.

4. After the soaking time has passed, beat the eggs in a large deep plate.

5. Heat plenty of oil in a large skillet over medium heat.

6. Drain the bread slices of excess milk and dredge them in beaten egg, making sure they are well coated on both sides.

7. Fry the torrijas in the hot oil until golden and crispy on both sides. Turn them so they brown evenly.

8. Once fried, place the torrijas on absorbent paper to remove excess oil.

9. Sprinkle sugar and cinnamon over the torrijas to taste.

10. Serve the torrijas hot or let them cool to room temperature. They can be eaten both hot and cold.

Enjoy these delicious torrijas, a classic of Spanish cuisine, especially popular at Easter and during the Christmas holidays!

DONUTS

Preparation time: 30 minutes

Servings: Varies depending on the size of the donuts

Ingredients:

- 500 g wheat flour
- 200g sugar
- 3 eggs
- 100ml milk
- 100 ml mild olive oil

- 1 sachet of chemical yeast (15 g)
- Zest of 1 lemon
- 1 pinch of salt
- Oil for frying
- Powdered sugar (optional, to decorate)

Preparation:

1. In a large bowl, mix the flour with the sugar, baking powder and a pinch of salt.
2. Add the lightly beaten eggs, milk, light olive oil and lemon zest to the flour mixture. Knead well until you obtain a soft and homogeneous dough.
3. Cover the dough with a clean cloth and let it rest for at least 30 minutes.
4. After the resting time, form the donuts. You can make small balls of dough and make

a hole in the center with your finger or use a mold to shape them.

5. Heat plenty of oil in a frying pan over medium-high heat. When the oil is hot, fry the donuts in batches until golden brown on both sides, about 3-4 minutes per side.

6. Once fried, remove the donuts from the oil with a slotted spoon and place them on absorbent paper to remove excess oil.

7. If you wish, you can dust the donuts with confectioners' sugar once they have cooled slightly.

8. Serve the donuts and enjoy them as a delicious dessert or traditional snack.

I hope you enjoy these tasty donuts, ideal for sharing on any occasion!

CHURROS WITH CHOCOLATE

Preparation time: 30 minutes

Servings: 4

Ingredients:

For the churros:

- 1 cup of water
- 2 tablespoons of sugar
- 1/2 teaspoon salt

- 2 tablespoons vegetable oil
- 1 cup of wheat flour
- Oil for frying

For the hot chocolate:

- 200 g dark chocolate
- 1 cup of milk
- 2 tablespoons sugar (optional)

Preparation:

1. In a medium pot, boil the water along with the sugar, salt and vegetable oil.
2. Remove the pot from the heat and add the wheat flour all at once. Mix quickly with a wooden spoon until you obtain a smooth and homogeneous dough.
3. Fill a pastry bag with the churros dough and place a star-shaped nozzle on the end.

4. Heat plenty of oil in a deep frying pan or deep fryer to 180°C (350°F).

5. Squeeze the dough directly into the hot oil, forming strips approximately 10-12 cm long. Cut the dough with scissors to separate the churros.

6. Fry the churros in batches until golden brown and crispy, about 2-3 minutes per side. Remove them from the oil and drain them on absorbent paper.

7. Meanwhile, prepare the hot chocolate. In a small saucepan, heat the milk over medium heat and add the chopped chocolate. Stir constantly until the chocolate is completely melted. If you want it sweeter, add the 2 tablespoons of sugar and mix well.

8. Serve the churros hot along with hot chocolate for dipping.

Enjoy these delicious churros with chocolate, a classic of Spanish pastries!

Printed in Great Britain
by Amazon

48312e94-f8e7-4efa-901e-4f540389b605R01